Empty Glasses
and
Empty Tables

Empty Glasses and Empty Tables

by

Luo Ying

DORRANCE PUBLISHING CO., INC.
PITTSBURGH, PENNSYLVANIA 15222

ISBN: 978-0-8059-7523-9
Library of Congress Control Number: 2006937122

Printed in the United States of America

First Printing

For more information or to order additional books, please contact:
Dorrance Publishing Co., Inc.
701 Smithfield Street
Third Floor
Pittsburgh, Pennsylvania 15222
U.S.A.
1-800-788-7654
www.dorrancebookstore.com

This book is dedicated to my lovely mother.

Loving life and protecting nature are characteristics of a good poet.

A Brief Introduction of Luo ying

 Luo Ying, the penname of Huang Nubo, is a new star with great talent in China's poetry circles in recent years. Born in Lanzhou, Gansu province, P.R.C., in 1956, five years later he moved to Yinchuan, Ningxia province, with his parents. He began to publish poetry in newspapers and periodicals at a very early age, and in 1976, was accepted as a student in the Chinese Department of Peking University under the tutorship of the renowned Professor Xie Mian. In August, 1992, the collection *Love Me No More* was published, followed by *No More Melancholy* in 1995, *The Fallen Petals* (160 poems) in July, 2003, and *Wandering in the Metropolis* (104 poems) in January, 2005. The last two collections have received much attention in that they signify the maturity of Luo Ying's poetry in that his rich social and cultural spirit is powerfully united with strong humanitarian concerns. *Wandering in the Metropolis,* a collection in which the flaws and shadows of modern urban life are profoundly reflected and revealed, has garnered much attention in poetry circles. In 2005, seminars on *Wandering* were held in cities such as Beijing, Shanghai, Guangzhou, Urmuqi, and so on, during which many famous poets and poetic critics showed their appreciation for the collection. One of them, Mr. Niu Han, a famous Chinese poet, even termed it "the Luo Ying phenomenon". In the summer of 2005, the organizing committee of "Our Culture", consisting of 13 governmental departments and societies, held a series of on-campus activities about Luo Ying's poetry, and organized several poetry recitals in universities in several cities, including Beijing, Guangzhou, and Shenzhen. In January, 2006, Mr. Luo Ying was engaged as an "ambassador" of the "2006 All China Poetry Movement" by the Chinese Poetry Society, and gave lectures in the U.S. in April under the invitation from the Asian Fund, U.S.A., the Asian Culture Association, U.S.A., and the Los Angeles Society of Chinese Writers in North America. September, 2006, saw the publication of *The Bunny*, another collection by Mr. Luo Ying, which consists of 10 poems, a preface and a postscript. With a new style, form and expressive force, this collection sees the poet's continue to analyze and critique the anti-humanitarianism of modern civilization, while delving more deeply into these issues and employing a different form than in his previous poetry.

Contents

Lou Ying Poetry Translations
by Michael Day

Preface 1

By Michael Martin Day

Huang Nubo, Chairman of the Board of Beijing's Zhongkun Investment Group, announced that the corporation will give 30 million Yuan to poetry activities: 10 million Yuan to the Beijing University New Poetry Research Institute; 10 million Yuan to the China Poetry Studies Association; and 10 million Yuan to establish a China Poetry Foundation (November 17, 2005).

I wrote this paragraph about three weeks ago as part of an annual review of notable events on the poetry scene in China for a Leiden University website. In October 2005, when my good friend Tang Xiaodu asked me to consider translating the poetry of a businessman-friend of his for money, my initial reaction was negative. I thought I didn't need the money that badly. I was quite busy, and the poetry wouldn't be as good as I'd like it to be (and if it was that good, I'd do it for free, as I so often do. But none of the poets I like have ever been in the happy situation of being able to offer me money—not that I would ask if they were). By December, however, my friendship with Xiaodu won me over: I trust him and his judgment and knew he wouldn't ask me to do anything that might embarrass me.

So in December, I wrote an email agreeing to translate the poetry of Luo Ying, the penname of the businessman Xiaodu had once or twice referred to as Mr. Huang, and thought nothing more of it...until I was asked to write this preface, and in so doing read the prefaces to Luo Ying's two published poetry collections. Then finally, the penny dropped, and I "recognized" Mr. Huang as the Huang Nubo I already "knew" and liked from the description above.

At this moment, I feel a bit foolish. My excuses for not knowing of Huang Nubo are my busy-ness, my temporary residence in remote Manchester, England, the fact that I haven't set foot in Beijing since the summer of 1994, and my current obsession with avant-garde poetry on the Internet in China. In any case, it is Luo Ying and his poetry I know well, and that is what I am going to write about here. Suffice it to say that Luo Ying was born into poverty in the countryside far from Beijing, and through hard work, opportunity, and intelligence—if not genius—he has transformed himself into what he is today: one of China's foremost business people and a poet who seeks to engage with society and, for the most part, succeeds in doing so.

Most of the poems collected here are from Luo Ying's second book: *The Roaming in the City Collection* (2005). His own words from the postscript to the book clearly set out the motivations for his poetry:

Poetry is a type of emotion.

I believe poetry is an art of appreciative observation and reflective testimony, an art of emotional outpouring, and an art of catharsis. We can use her to express love, hatred, complaint, or criticism, while hoping to rouse a sympathetic response....

It's impossible to imagine a poet only being able to complain to himself under a lamp; and it's also impossible to imagine a poet not being influenced in any way by present-day society...Admittedly, we oppose the concept of class struggle and don't think poetry ought to bear the heavy responsibility of social criticism, or simply become a political noise, and yet poetry is a special art, it is the cream of the arts....

My poetry does not want to overthrow the city, instead it is a thirst for social conscience, a thirst for social justice, and this can be considered an attitude to life of mine. I am a direct beneficiary of urbanization. When standing atop a skyscraper looking back or gazing down on so many people from out of town and those beneath the building, all still located on another of life's horizons, can you say there's something not right about poetry beginning to weep and critique?

When I finally came out of The Roaming in the City Collection, *escaped from this mood of grief and indignation, my spirit returned to peace, my thoughts became rational, and my poetical emotions were calm once more....*

Luo Ying truly does roam the city in his poetry, wandering the streets and lobbies of the skyscrapers that crowd the city and help to alienate him from both the city and its crowds. Windows in his poetry are seldom transparent views on the soul, unless they are glimpses on the anguished mind of the poet and his reflections on the images he sees through them and on them. The climate in his city is cold, dehumanizing, and mal-formed by the geography, and this is set off against occasional forays into the nearby dreary suburbs. Escape is imaginative, a function of the mem-ory of life before the city in a distant, true home. But the memory is always vague, if not resonant.

Luo's situation as a country boy now making a home in a strange and estranging city is far from novel, as it is shared by tens of millions of oth-ers like him who have moved into the cities of China to chase jobs and dreams since the early 1980s. Luo is one of the lucky few, meeting as he has with enormous, if not ironic, success as a property developer, an urban-izer par excellence. These poems give full reign to his repugnance for certain aspects of city life, from the hallucinatory nature of clubbing to the difficulties of interpersonal contact and communication.

There may be little that is new in this subject matter, but a collection devoted almost exclusively to such poetry is novel. Among modern poets, praise or criticism of the modernity of the city is often balanced against praise or criticism of the bucolic pleasures and non-modern aspects of country life. A common poetical subject is that of an idealized form of rural paradise set in the distant past—a everpresent staple of Chinese poetry, both classical and modern. Fittingly Luo makes use of modernist poetical techniques when they suit his purpose, and the aesthetic of ugli-ness seems to inform much of his work here. As the words of his post-script indicate, strong emotion permeates his work. There is sympathy for insects and glimpsed passersby and flashes of striking lyrical beauty. To this end, a number of poems from his earlier collection have not only been selected as leavening agents but also to illustrate that Luo is not a one-note poet, forever harping on about the unhappiness he witnesses and experiences.

Classical imagery and parallelism recur frequently in Luo's poems, as does rhyme. This last aspect is untranslatable and thus gives the poetry translated here more of a "modern" feel than is the case in the Chinese. The end-rhyme of –ang is a clear favorite of the poet. The sound of it is resonant of the rumbling of traffic and the monotonous low-level hum-ming of machinery, so prevalent that longtime city dwellers rarely notice it. In the Chinese language, this sound is also linked to feelings of pain and sorrow: the character for hurt is "shang" and appears in a number of collocations, such as "bei-shang," meaning sorrow; China's sorrow is the Huang He or Yellow River and so on.

Huang's rootless roaming amid the concrete and steel of the city calls to mind the ancient poet Qu Yuan (c. B.C. 40, B.C. 278), famous for his roaming through the state of Chu after being exiled by his king for speaking painful truths. Moreover this poet and his famous poem, "Encountering Sorrow," is consciously mimicked by Luo Ying in poem number twenty-five of the series "Songs of Roaming in the City."

Finally, it is of interest to note that the poet's penname, Luo Ying, shares the identical sounds and the second character of a still frequently used classical poetry collocation meaning "falling blossoms," which are reminiscent of the fleeting nature of life and beauty, if not the beauty of death itself. On the other hand, the poet's given name, Huang Nubo, can be translated as Yellow Angry Wave, which is the sort of penname one might expect from poets belonging to the "popular" or "among the people" tendency of post-1980 avant-garde poets. This seeming contradiction is also present in the poetry collected here. Given the poet's background and present status, the absence of such contradictions would be a surprise indeed, and I believe that knowledge of this background and status will add to the readers' enjoyment and experience of the poems collected here.

March 23, 2006

Michael Martin Day

 Michael Martin Day was born and educated in Vancouver, Canada. He received his BA in Asian Studies and the Chinese Language from the University of British Columbia (UBC) in 1985 and his MA in Modern Chinese Literature from the same university in 1994. Between the years of 1982 and 1992, he spent seven years in China, first as a cultural exchange scholarship student at the universities of Shandong and Nanjing, then as a teacher of English language and literature in Zhanjiang and Xi'an, and later as a journalist and editor in Beijing and Hongkong. He began teaching the Chinese language as an assistant lecturer at UBC in 1986 and later served in the same position for courses in Modern Chinese Literature in Chinese and A General Introduction to East Asian History and Culture. In 1995 and 1996, he was lecturer in charge of the Chinese Language Summer Program at the University of Lethbridge in Alberta, Canada. Between 2000 and 2005, he worked at Charles University, Prague, as a parttime lecturer of Modern Chinese Poetry. Advanced Chinese (Analysis of the Writings

of Mao Zedong), Academic English, and Poetry Translation. In 2002 he entered the Doctoral program at the University of Leiden, the Netherlands, as a long-distance student under the supervision of Professor Maghiel van Crevel. In September 2003, he was awarded a CCK Foundation Doctoral Dissertation Fellowship, which made the writing of his doctoral thesis possible, and completed his doctorate in October 2005 on the subject of the development of avant-garde poetry in Sichuan province during the 1980s. He has published several English language translations of Chinese poetry and fiction in Canada, the USA, the UK, and the Netherlands, as well as articles on Chinese poetry and politics in the Czech Republic, Hongkong, and China (prior to 1989).

Preface 2
No Longer a Shared Search but a Mutual Discovery

—On reading Luo Ying's Roaming in the City

by Tang Xiaodu
(Translated by Michael M. Day)

Following the publication of *Roaming in the City* in 2005, a reporter from *The New Beijing Post* interviewed me by phone. Afterwards she asked me whether I felt Luo Ying's poetry was somewhat confrontational. I asked her in what way and she said, "He is a big businessman but curses the city. Isn't that confrontational?" Apparently in the eyes of that reporter, it was okay for poets to curse the city, but a big boss should not. And why? Because if you're a big boss, you're a promoter and beneficiary of the city and urbanization; profiting from the city and then cursing it fits nicely with the saying "getting an advantage and then flaunting one's cleverness" and is therefore confrontational. She found it impossible to harmonize the positions of Huang Nubo the big boss and Luo Ying the poet and felt perplexed by the split, even the mutual antagonism, between the two.

We could say this reporter's understanding of the poet's position is too simple, too superficial, but we should not be overly critical of her, as her opinion reflects that of the common man and is a commonly held opinion.

By comparison, it is the standpoint of the "expert view" that is a problem. This viewpoint has it that for "an entrepreneur, writing like this is not bad." It sounds very broadminded but in its bones is even less genuine: aesthetically lowering the standard in pursuit of the disingenuous and in so doing being even more disingenuous in concealing the crux of the problem.

At the time, I said to the reporter that we were possibly looking at a unique case of a split, with the "split" here not only touching on the poet's position, or status, but on a deeper level, indicative of the split between a person's heart and mind, or between the left and the right hand. It is on this level that we should understand Luo Ying when he says in his poetry, "I'm me/and I am not me." This type of split is unrelated to getting an advantage or flaunting one's cleverness. And I am afraid it is also very difficult to "harmonize." What it makes starkly apparent is an existential condition of modern humanity and the internal state of modern poetry as well.

Could it be that this split embodies an "anti-modernist modernism"? There are two modernisms present here. The first is the modernism that began with the industrial revolution and accompanied the processes of industrialization and urbanization, all the way up to current "globalization." In the words of Octavio Paz, this modernism is a form of universal pursuit.

A recent film by the talented young Chinese director Jia Zhangke is called *The World.* Set against the background of globalization, this film features a unique Chinese perspective of contemporary life, in particular the everyday life on the lowest rungs of society in China. More to the point, it pops a beautiful illusory bubble. The conclusion of the film is both tragic and perplexing: After repeated failures, the main male and female characters are able to borrow a friend's apartment and it seems they're will spend their days together in mutual solace, but then it seems that after carrying out a certain ritual, they are bound to part. The next morning, however, they are both discovered to have died of gas poisoning. Nobody knows if this conclusion was an accident or a pact born of their mutual despair. Yet this is not important, as the new world that twinkled before them, as if on the horizon like a secret promise to the main characters and everybody else, that tempted them to turn their backs on family and hometown and did not spare the fatal blow, is entirely indifferent to their plight. An invisible hand manipulates our collective desire to rush to it, and innumerable such urges steer the so-called "wheel of history." But as far as this wheel is concerned, to what does the death of two day-laborers amount?

Giving such a film the title of *The World* is highly significant. As a prospect, this "world" could be called "the China dream," and behind it hides the ancient idea of "utopia," even though this utopia is exposed in an anti-utopian way. In the past, our so-called utopia always had the poetic flavor of fields and gardens, but today, against the backdrop of globalization, the pursuit of this form of modernism has led to its sudden disappearance and replacement by the city, a new poeticism, and its signifiers. The city is both our place of dreams and the path by which we realize our dreams, but it is also the place where we are lost and the gathering place where this loss leads to disillusionment. Yet no matter how lost and disillusioned we may become, the pursuit of this modernism is, at least at the moment, still an irresistible tide. The increased pace of urbanization is causing the city itself, even reality (including our internal reality) to become increasingly like Kafka's castle. The result is its mazy nature is not only located in its incomprehensibility and indecipherability, but also in the vacant position of the main actor, in the inability to promulgate commands, aside from the "new jungle of regulations" that are tacitly approved of, but which in the name of accumulating wealth and happiness leads us to descend into a common madness. Faced with the daily expansion of the city, with these jungles of reinforced concrete, those grotesque, ever-changing illusions on our screens, and the innumerable deep-seated, unfathomable transactions and conspiracies between those illusions, who could be rash enough to foster any thoughts of being a "main actor"?

From ordinary city people to serious, sincere high government officials, from casual laborers in ragged clothes to dignified CEOs in their suits, from the jokey mass media to the serious mouthpieces of the Communist Party, it seems all people acknowledge and follow the dictates of a higher existence, a nameless, dehumanized, irresponsible, uncontrollable power, the influence and peremptoriness of which is like some ancient amulet or some other form of contemporary totalitarianism. Of course, we all know the theory of "alienation" of Hegel and the young Marx, yet this does not prevent us, however unwillingly, from being manipulated by this alien power. Just as urges, capital, and might are united in this power, our helplessness in the throes of its manipulation features a mixture of being subject to cruelty and practicing it as well. So our asymmetrical situation forces us to pay a price day after day and, as if kidnapped, the injury it inflicts on people, human nature, the entirety of the world, and the life of the individual is accepted as unavoidable fate. This fate determines and incessantly re-determines the role of each individual, and ultimately we discover that all roles are actually the same role, which is to be a day-laborer for this form of modernism—for here differing "status" is leveled, returned to its original state in which all of modern humanity finds itself in an identical condition.

To a large degree, this is also the state of modern poetry: the difference being that poetry rose up in revolt against this condition from the start and in so doing defined "modernism" in poetry. In other words, from the very beginning, modernism in poetry embodied a querying and criticism of the aforementioned modernism. Generally speaking, we can say this is a dual refusal of difference, of two parallel modernisms, and in its extreme sense, it can also be said that the latter modernism is a type of "anti-modernist modernism."

Some western scholars trace modernism in poetry back to early romanticism, and I see this as particularly necessary. It cannot be said that there is some essential characteristic that links modern poetry, in its broad sense, from that time to this (I do not wish to fall into such an essentialist trap; furthermore, there are poetical phenomena that require concrete analysis, such as the modernist disorientation of futurism and Sandburg's praise of industrialization and urbanization), but a skeptical and critical spirit is doubtless its living soul. This principle is similarly applicable to itself, and in this the secret of why—and at an identical speed to the aforementioned modern socioeconomic change as well—modern poetry rigorously enforced transformations on itself. According to my understanding, it was precisely due to this particular internal need that Rimbaud appealed, "We must modernize, must modernize absolutely!"

As it is, I myself have been working toward this end all along. At the same time, I hope this sort of parallel description and separating of modernisms provides a textual background that makes interpretation of Luo Ying's poetry possible, just as I hope it will also be of assistance in clarifying the poetical lineage to which he belongs.

As far as contemporary Chinese poetry is concerned, recently arisen "urban poetry" and "day-worker poetry" also belongs to this line and, if necessary, can be traced to Shu Ting's early-1980s poem, "The Assembly Line," which was the earliest contemporary poem to touch on the subject of "alienation." This poem was severely criticized upon publication with the result that to this day, it remains the lone example of this genre in her oeuvre. Of course, such a positioning does not weaken the unique value and significance of Luo Ying. Scope is one aspect; another is that no matter the depth or breadth the subject may achieve, it is in his experimentation with form that he provides sufficient new things. His best-written works feature keen experiential settings, a strict aesthetic vision, a sense of loss resulting from continuous reassessment, and a process of abstract dramatization that organically fuses it all together. Stylistically his poetry is lucid and lively; situations are as clearly depicted it seems they are before our eyes, and this helps highlight his field of discourse and does not hinder possible ambiguous and variable interpretations. See, for example, *Empty Glasses and Empty Tables:*

Glass / Opposes glass / The tables/Quiet as autumn leaves falling to earth / The fragrance of wine dregs spreads / Like a girl leaving after a hot kiss / Glass after glass / Deliberates on the emptiness / The tables/Cleaned by drizzle / Cannot sing / And don't fear being dirtied by wind / Year on year the frosts always come / Night on night the wine will always be drunk / Glass will always / Oppose glass

A still life, yet filled by a massive "emptiness."

This poem can be seen as a depiction of an immediate time and place and as a portrait of a final phase of life, or the world as well. The lines "Glass after glass / Deliberates on the emptiness" are of particular significance. Due to this "glass," the unsubstantial, formless, ungraspable "emptiness" not only achieves an illusory quantification but also simultaneously achieves an auditory sense, a sense of taste, and tactile sensation through the mutual correlation of the quiet as autumn leaves fall to earth, the dispersing of the fragrance of the wine dregs, and the passionate kiss of the girl as she leaves. Moreover, "deliberates" also provides it with unremitting temporal and spatial aspects. Conversely through this "deliberation" and the linkage of the two "always" lines at the end of the stanza, what appears between the first lines, "Glass / Opposes glass," and the final lines, "Glass will always / Oppose glass," is far from just a cyclical or progressive association achieved through a change in rhetoric, for it also simultaneously introduces self-mockery, irony, helplessness, and so on, and weaves all this together into an even more complex mood.

At the very least, the "empty" in *Empty Glasses and Empty Tables* contains the meanings of "hollow" and "open and quiet," and also hints at an identical reality: that of the absence (emptiness and nothingness) of "man." I believe this is the nodal point that both connects and separates Huang Nubo the entrepreneur and Luo Ying the poet, as well as the omnipresent wanderer in *Roaming the City*—the jumping-off point of "I."

And from here, he brings us one whirlwind of language after another, which passes through squares and skyscrapers, loiters in alleys and on street corners, dances through rooms and drawers, now hot, now cold, one moment full of the worries of the world, and the next treats it with nothing but cynicism. There is catharsis and revelation, exposure and critique, including self-criticism. This criticism is seldom direct; it is interior and encompasses social critiques, systemic critiques, and critiques of civilization. As it employs a higher criterion—the criterion of poetry—from the start, it integrates the aesthetic criteria of life, the soul, emotions, and dreams. It is a holistic principle of the "Being" of man (Heidigger's "Sein"), which is being lost or abandoned by even more people and is therefore a criterion that must be particularly safeguarded.

If it can be said that the "city" in this poetry collection symbolizes this aforementioned nameless, dehumanized, irresponsible, uncontrollable power and the injury it causes—encirclement, isolation, deformation, objectification, absurdity, loneliness, phoniness, indifference, rupture, being replicated, a leveling out, fabrication, and so on—if this has formed the destiny of the individual, then "roaming" is symbolic of resistance, a counter-making and a transcendence of this power, this sort of injury, and this type of destiny.

This meaning of "roaming" is similar to the older poet Niu Han's "dream-wandering." In *A Secret Flight in Another World—Niu Han and His "Dream-Wandering,"* I attempted to define "dream-wandering." Firstly, after undergoing deformation, it is the tortuous realization on earth of the urge to fly; secondly, besides beetles, under the great pressure of huge rocks we have the possibility of becoming another type of humankind; thirdly, it is a symbolic prison break, and fourthly, we arrive in another world via extraordinary measures. At least the first three of these are fundamentally applicable to Luo Ying's "roaming." As to why there are reservations over the fourth, I would prefer to reply with a line from a poem by the Greek poet Elytis: "This, ah, this world, it's the same world."

Of course, to a poet, no matter how great the aspiration or how profound the thought, if he cannot transform the stimuli of his personal experience into an appropriate form and on this basis produce a unique voice, it all becomes no more than empty words. In an information rich age, such as today's, this is even more the case.

This is a process from search to discovery. Compare *Roaming in the City* with *Falling Flowers,* published two years earlier, and a similar process can be clearly observed in the author's mental and physical efforts. For the most part, the linguistic posturing in *Falling Flowers* was a type of "proper lyricism," and this brought with it a closed-off poeticism and a relatively unitary style: romantic, gentle, adjusted and decorative, aesthetic, a refined melancholy, and a concentration of harmless uncertainty and time passing like a song. Moreover, whether or not the writer was conscious of it, there was a substantial imitative element in all these poems. On the other hand, at the same time as *Roaming in the City* opens toward other possible poeticisms (including so-called "anti-poeticism"), it draws together many more elements that are poetical: elements of a differing nature that not only merge together but break each other apart. As a result, a merging of styles was created, to such a degree that it occasionally verges on the barbaric, until it gave me the illusion that it seemed that in moving from *Falling Flowers* to *Roaming in the City,* the history of contemporary Chinese poetry was reenacted in a synchronic manner in the writing of one person. Is this a sign of maturity? No. I am more inclined to say this is an indication of a fertile vitality. And without such vitality, creativity loses its foundation.

Observed from the perspective of sound, or musicality, the poetry of *Roaming in the City* is far richer and more complex than that of *Falling Flowers.* Some poems, such as "Midnight Letters Home" and "Drawers," preserve the former gentle lyrical tone, but there is greater tension and a greater sense of decorum. Others of these poems possess an obviously more prominent element of rhythm. Their songlike nature requires a different form of singing, such as "On the Road," which I fear is better suited to the rap form. While being interviewed by *The New Beijing Post,* when I summed up the particular characteristics of the sounds in *Roaming in the City* as incisive, severe, and desolate, I was primarily referring to these poems. In *Falling Flowers,* this sort of sound was rarely in evidence and not just because of differences in source materials and subject matter. A poem by Luo Ying can probably better illustrate the problem. In this particular case, a tireless inquisition is ultimately taken as the title of the poem, and what he inquires into is: Who truly exists?

And this is also the reason I set greater store by a different type of poem as represented by the sequences "Impressions" and "Impressions of Me on Myself." In these poems, the songlike aspect at which Luo Ying is so skilled is comprehensively subverted, and the rhythm becomes particularly succinct and compelling. The usual poetic line is no longer present, and all that remains is a string of characters and words cut into their smallest units, at most a few brief words. It cannot be said that there are no linguistic links between them, but this type of arrangement, the special method of reading it requires, the unexpected and loosely logical linkages in the jumps from one linguistic unit to another, and the vast void that is created by this form of leap brings to the fore a sense of drunken, bleary-eyed discontinuity, something between talking in one's sleep and aphasia. These single characters and words do not seem to come from a pen but from a previously schematic-ised pressure unit; they are not written out but are sprayed, or dropped, onto the page. A void that spreads out endlessly in all directions, cut off from previous and later text, makes them appear many times more unusual, strange, isolated, and abrupt. Previously unseen in Luo Ying's writing, this linguistic phenomenon and its form is particularly eye-catching, and the arbitrary and forceful nature of it, like a soldering gun suddenly roaring to life beside one on a dark night, is startling. Take as an example "Impressions: Pets":

Like me / By / The city / Reared in a pen / A metallic / Hatred / Fantasies / Like horse piss / Every day / Wanting / To shatter / Sunlight / Behind / The back / Of the curses / Of time pieces / Naked / Casting off / Candlelight/Like lead wire / Like/Seamless lightning / Rolling past / Then / Melting into / A soup of mud

Or "Impressions of Me on Myself: # 11":

Like / A / Faded / Painting / Fixed / On / A wall / The manner in which / The wind blows / Odd / And / Hard to dodge / Bare-bottomed / Nails / Pester me / Beams of light / Like/Airborne blades / Fly in / Upside down / A one-eyed / Person / Enters / And is then / Easily / Imprisoned / My faded color / Revolts against / My/Motley shade / The rain / Comes down so / It makes/The heart race

The texture of this type of poetry is a combination of the strangeness of titanium alloy, the cold rigidity of reinforced concrete, and the magic of the flickering of neon lights. If when reading this poetry, besides the predicament of being left breathless, you sometimes can sense the staccato bursts of a happy lack of inhibition. This is because you, like the author, are simultaneously taking on the roles of the marksman and the bull's eye. I know that when faced with this type of poetry, the majority of people will consider influences; similarly I know this is precisely Luo Ying's expression of a greater originality and therefore these are poems that are truly his—they are destined to be attained once and then mutually forsaken. As they can only be produced at moments that can only be met and not pursued, at such moments, existence, form, and the poet are no longer in a shared search but in a mutual discovery.

Tang Xiaodu

Tang Xiaodu, critic and poet, was born in 1954 in Yizheng, Jiangsu Province. After graduating from the Nanjing University in 1981, he first worked as an editor of *Poetry Monthly* in Beijing and now works as a senior editor at The Writers Publishing House. He is a member of the Chinese Writers Association; a council member of the Chinese New Poetry Institute; a research fellow at the New Poetry Research Center, Beijing University; and a concurrent professor at the Hainan University.

For over twenty years, Tang has mainly devoted himself to researching, criticizing, and compiling the Chinese contemporary poetry, especially poetry of avant-garde. He has published four collections of essays, including *Starting Points Anew Constantly* (1989), *Tang Xiaodu on Poetry: A Selection* (1993), *Close-readings on the Masterpieces of the World Modern Poetry* (1998), and *Anthology of Tang Xiaodu's Essays on Poetry* (2001). He translated and published The Art of Novel, written by Milan Kundera (1993), and also translated many foreign poets' works into Chinese, such as Sylvia Plath, Vaclaw Havel, Czeslaw Milosz, Zbigniew Herbert, Miroslav Holub, etc. He edited and co-edited numerous poetry anthologies, and his own work is also anthologized both at home and abroad. He was the recipient of the Wenyi Zhengming Award for Criticism and the Shanhua Award for Literal Theory in 1995 and was twice awarded Modern Writers Review Prize for criticism in 2004 and 2005.

Tang has been a frequent guest to the international poetry conference and festivals since the mid-1990s. Between 1995 and 2002, he made his literal appearances at Leiden University, London University, Brown University, Harvard University, and universities in France and Czech.

Preface 3
Destined to Roam

Shuntarô Tanikawa

I read *Roaming in the City* in the Japanese version with occasional references to the English version. When I first met the author, Luo Ying, in my house, I was presented with the Chinese original book, but on the calling card he game me, I saw "Huang Nubo," not "Luo Ying" printed as his name. When I met him the second time in China on invitation, I felt more intimacy toward the earthly work of Huang rather than toward Luo Ying's work on paper. The two names "Luo Ying" and "Huang Nubo" are too intricately intertwined with each other and in places too closely coalesce to be called a penname and a real name. That's the impression I got from this book of poems.

A poem called "Living" ends with the following two lines: "Living is/ to clench teeth and swear not to speak of pain." There are metaphors and rhetoric in the lines preceding this, but in these two lines we hear the author's urgent voice that says, "No time for poetic rhetoric!" The prologue of "Impressions of Me on Myself" contains: "I'm me/And I am not me." It seems this poet is trying hard to take contradictions upon himself, not to deceive himself about ambivalence, and so to integrate himself into a deeper, multivocal vessel."

As businessman Huang Nubo, he plays an important part in the expansion of the city. As poet Luo Ying, he rejects the city and is rejected by the city. The relationship between him and the city is a subtle affair that cannot be settled by a mere love-hate resolution. That the word "Roam" is the keyword he must be fully aware. The relationship is always on the move. The poet Luo Ying is roaming not just in the city. He is destined to roam between the abstract world of language and the concreteness of land, between cynicism and romanticism, between the city and frontiers.

There is something pathetic and dramatic about his roaming, which I think gives a peculiar tone to the style of his poetry, but the man I actually see before me is a tall sportsman with a mild smile. Though not included in the English version, there is a poem called "Criticism of Economics" in the Japanese version, probably published simultaneously. "I think / that I am a volume of *Criticism of Economics.* /I write poetry in order to shed light /upon the wreath which burglars have stolen...."

I regret that I can't quote the whole of this excellent piece, but behind the frank theme and the outspoken tone is hidden a soul which proves that Luo Ying and Huang Nubo are never separate persons but are one personality living in the contemporary age. There is no doubt that this book of poems is one of the fresh fruits produced out of the almost fearful energy of Modern China's economy and culture.

August 2006
Translated by William I. Elliott and Kazuo Kawamura

Shuntarô Tanikawa

Shuntarô Tanikawa, born in 1931 in Tokyo, the only child of well-known philosopher Tetsuzô Tanikawa, is among the most popular contemporary poets in Japan. After finishing high school, he decided not to go on to a university. His first book of poems, *Two Billion Light-Years of Solitude,* appeared in 1952. He has since produced some seventy books of poetry and won every major Japanese award for his writing. He has also written essays, radio and film scripts, and picture books for children. He is the translator of the Mother Goose rhymes and has for many years been the translator of *Peanuts.* He has performed his poems in America, Ireland, England, and China. His books of poems that have so far been translated into English are *Two Billion Light-Years of Solitude* (trans.1996), *62 Sonnets* (1953, trans. 1992), *On Love* (1955, trans. 2003), *With Silence My Companion* (1968, trans. 1975), *At Midnight in the Kitchen I Just Wanted to Talk to You* (1975, trans. 1980), *Definitions* (1975, trans. 1992), *Coca-Cola Lessons* (1980, trans. 1986), *Map of Days* (1982, trans. 1996), *Songs of Nonsense* (1985, trans. 1991), *Floating the River in Melancholy* (1988, trans. 1988), *Naked* (1988, trans. 1996), *On Giving People Poems* (1991, trans. 2005), *The Naif* (1993, trans. 2004) and *minimal* (2002, trans. 2002). *The Selected Poems of*

Shuntarô Tanikawa was published in America in 1983. *Shuntarô Tanikawa: Selected Poems* was published by Carcanet, U.K., in 1998. His most recent book of poems is *SUKI* (*Liking*), published in May 2006.

Roaming in the City

A clear morning
I want to start to roam
The sunlight's in a fright
I worry for the worm in the concrete crack
How will she face the blazing sun of today
The returned night loses her gentle cry
And my rambling will surely lose its way in this city
Grass on the corner, you'll wither
Heavy steps are sure to break your back
Naked sleep through the eternal night is not as sweet as you
This night's dreams are sure to be wild
Homeless dog, are you still watching over me
Waiting on me to beg scraps of sausage for you
Waiting for that worry-free sparrow to alight on your back
Singing and flying on a whim

People
This tie's like a yoke, strapping me into this prison cell of a city
My spirit roams among the skyscrapers
Every glance both indifferent and a thirst
Every door makes me vacillate
I can't penetrate this shimmering glass
Like steel cables, the network of wires tightly trusses my mind
My hand grips coffee and my heart is sad
And my birthplace, your streams still run for me

Urban Cockroaches

This pack of vehicles sweeps over the city like cockroaches
Each street like a black snake on the wing
Confronting each other through car windows,
are people similarly desolate
As if in prison wagons being driven to a wrestling ring
The city's ring road   aah truly a magnetic field
Nobody is allowed to flee the city
This city's cars   aah really like cockroaches
Rolling forward none willing to give way
The flashing police light seems to cry
Confused like a frantically scurrying rat

The Bridge

The bridge
Slowly stretches out in the setting sun
My love has vanished on the horizon
Shouts become blue
Like a skyscraper never again to move
Wind comes
Rain falls
Leaving me on the bridge, softly chanting
Every day the cacophony of this city makes me jumpy
Every night the distant desolation brings me fear
That far-traveling love makes my heart hurt
Yet this concrete bridge pens me in tight
Always moving right
Always spinning in place
Like the grass beneath the bridge
Forever in position bearing roots
If you say it's death, it's death
Say it's life, it's life
My love
Please take care

Midnight Letters Home

Midnight
Wanting to write a distant childhood
Outside the window
Returning car lights like fluttering threads of red
And it's the rushing
That's made me old and grave
A sleepless night
Like a trapped beast silent in a pit
The wind blows
Will the dawn bring an eyeful of drifting dead leaves
The roar of the river of cars is the sound of autumn
Half the city under thin frost
Half in silence
Who murmurs in a dream
Just like that childhood hometown sound
The heart moistens
The night is deep

Tonight I'm on the Net

Autumn rain has just wet the rising night
And I'm racing on the freeway of the World Wide Web
I want to know the direction from which the wind will come
Tonight what kind of face will I have
For a distant somebody raising a coffee
Who will savor my fragrance
Sliding on a notional pond like the sign of a mouse
Weave emotion into stormy waves with a program
Make moonlight with paper
Make sun with a lamp
Make a red bridal chamber with Mars
Speak to yourself of parting
Cry to yourself at sorrow
Like a lone wolf in the forest, wander on the internet
Like a camel free of the herd, search for pasturage
This keyboard ultimately cannot strike on my home
Tonight
I'm on the net

Wild Mushrooms by the Roadside

Sunlight
Also shines on the roadside
Under a locust tree
Like me wild mushrooms appear
Snuggling up beside the crowd
Facing the crowd
Not knowing when
Ground to pieces underfoot
The city's rain
Icy and flavorless
Coldly falls
Flying horizontal in February
Umbrellas raised
Yet no one wipes my tears

Windows

A window
Refracted by a window
A window
Hidden by a window
Warmth cut off by a window
Facing a window
Eyes alarmed in a window
Windows like the eyes of nocturnal wolves in a wood
Make the skyscrapers in the windows coldly flash
The windows of the buildings are like one-way mirrors
The me in the windows is stripped of my last clothes
You cannot smash each window
The window leaves you helpless and naked
A window
Confined by a window
A window
Watched by a window

KTV

Singing against oneself
Please turn up the echo
Like a mountain goat
Climbing a precipice to face a wolf
Like strong liquor
Eyes bamboozled by the last glass
Both wind and rain will be sung
Aah, villages
Please don't sparkle
Those days of autumn harvest like the chimes of a bell
Repeatedly stir the heart
That tryst by a stream like wild grass
In the heart, withering and flourishing again and again
The disco
Renders all chaos
A door opens
Little flower girl
You bring the initial smell of the rose of youth

Wrong Number

Dialed wrongly repeatedly
In a space of concrete
Thoughts are screened
A digital confusion
Nobody hears my call
My days are always offline
At all turns a dead machine
A dark screen night leaves one isolated
The heart will cry softly for grief
I don't know who will hear over there by the wall
A wrong number
As if I'm lost in the streets

Streetlights

Streetlights
Come shine on me
Tonight
I'll get deeply drunk
Shocked people
Get away from me quickly
These streets
Have untamed me
It's impossible to run wild
Every street is the same
People on the road
Always rushing
Men indifferent
Women cold
Nobody attends to me
A clinging shadow
Ask the wind to blow me
I'll not sway
And won't make a sound
Used to trifling days
Who will want to resist again
Like small flowers in the corners of walls living and dying
Withering when it's time to wither
Flourishing when time to flourish
Dusk
And I see children returning again

Gloomy Time

Nobody will play the lute before my window
My mailbox is always as empty as dreams
The setting sun stares at the street
but doesn't see my shadow
At dawn I smile to myself
When I think nobody will hear
Late at night I drink with myself
Momentarily stunned at being ripped apart
Each pair of eyes makes me anxious
On this road every person is in a dubious rush
Each vehicle seems about to crush my chest
These streets are as hot as walls of flame
Every brick is painfully scorched by the lights
Not daring to groan
I creep among the buildings
Each doorway is strange
This long night's ramble
Makes one feel bitter
This long night's sleeplessness
Makes one boundlessly sad
The eternal night of this city is too cold
The road home is already covered by frost and snow
This pained poem is passed on by nobody
Silently reciting lines walking the streets
Searching out and scrutinizing every street sign
Which stop
Is my first home

Neighbors

Neighbors
Are another door
The master of another dog

Neighbors
Are another mailbox
The owner of another door code

Neighbors
Are another seat on a bus
The owner of another digital watch

A Pond outside the City

A strand
Of setting sun
Stirs the pond
Into a coppery yellow
Withered leaves
Tossing
Waft over
Or
Fall on water
Wild lotuses
Are drifting
Lazily
And reveal
A partial stretch of red radiance
A bridge
Furtively appears
Penning in the city
On that side
This spring warmth
Outside the city
Comes again
Making lips tremble
Dusk
Spreads
Clouding
The eyes

Empty Glasses and Empty Tables

Glass
Opposes glass
The tables
Quiet as autumn leaves falling to earth
The fragrance of wine dregs spreads
Like a girl leaving after a hot kiss
Glass after glass
Deliberates on the emptiness
The tables
Cleaned by drizzle
Cannot sing
And don't fear being dirtied by wind
Year on year the frost always come
Night on night the wine will always be drunk

Glass will always
Oppose glass

Digital Camera

You
Will be repeatedly scrubbed out
Like mud
Simply wiped flat

You
Will be repeatedly invented
Like snow
Leaving no trace after the fall

You
Will be repeatedly compiled
And like paper
Ripped away piece by piece

You
Will repeatedly smile
And like a tree
Be skinned again and again

You
Will be saved without limit
Like a maggot
Squirming in black quartz

A Fabricated Marriage

Skyscraper after skyscraper
     Like beds
Standing vertical
     Rocking
From behind a window
     I spy
Curtains
     Like red underpants
Lamplight
     The network starts to brighten
     Fabricating at lightning speed
Hands
     Like trees waving in confusion
The heart
     Like the startling tones of a gong
Like dead leaves
     Late at night, slipping onto the streets
     Tossed about by the wind
Like winter snow
     At noon leaving traces on roofs
     Silently shooting back at the sunlight
This night
     Will fall ten thousand times
     Be used ten thousand times like Chanel No 5
Spying and being espied, ten thousand times
Free and allowed freedom, ten thousand times
In the indulgent night forced to wander
This city seems wrapped in a large condom
The sperm of this millennium will be shot in a night
This street full of men and women is fabricated by a suspicious marriage
Fabricated people
I see
The full moon over the bridge is true red

Ecstasy

Driven into a corner
      By the night
Yelling fiercely
      At smoke
Heavy metal music like a bastard
      Like a four-tooth saw blade
      Ripping the heart to pieces
      The DJ smashes plates with a horsewhip
I really want
      To break his hand
As if suddenly forced to change gender
      My night
      Abruptly reverses direction
      Into day
Just like a glacier gradually broken by the pressure of snow
      My boat
      Sinks into the abyss
      Shattered oars and broken masts
The eyes
      Can't clearly see eyes
How can this heart
      Not go wild
I don't know
      Who will forcibly occupy
My bed
      Who will be spared
The murder of this night

      An ecstasy tablet
The gonad of a bastard

Songs of Roaming in the City
(A Sequence of Thirty Poems)

#1

Dawn
Severed by a suspension bridge
Chaos
It's the wind that blows me
But doesn't
Carry off my clothes
Majestic steel buildings overlook me
Staggering
I can't find a vision to stand up to mine
Can't remember
Whose window I should knock on
Like going upstream in a mountain creek
Sunlight
Finally arrives
But is shattered by a million windows
Vaporized into a million rays of light

#2

Aah, city
Please let me roam the streets
Fluttering about at will
Like a scrap of paper
Crawling by the side of a ditch
Like a beetle
Night and day flying round a streetlight
Like a moth
Not wanting people to pay attention to
My careless death
The disorder of life wearies me
The monotony of roaming worries me
Aah, city
How should I decant this heartbreak

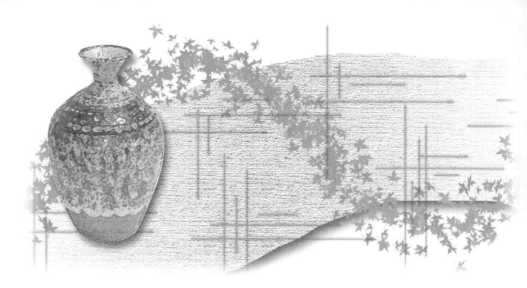

#3

Not daring to gaze into the distance
Hidden in sorrow behind the window of a skyscraper
The wind repeatedly raises remote roads
But the heart flees inward layer by layer
A sumptuous dressing gown cannot bear the cold frost
Deeply drunk eyes can't discern the direction
A thorough soaking of rain will give me palpitations
The foot-piercing thorns will cause me deep regrets
Over the great desert alarm signals of smoke will leave me helpless
And the bleakness of the wilds will make me panic
Aah tall buildings
Why do you hem me in so tight

#4

Morning star
You ascend so uselessly
This city's night and day are similarly bright
I've long since lit every light in every street
And those that wouldn't light are the routes of my laborious roaming
I will abruptly drop like an autumn leaf
But can't easily dissolve into dust
I will suddenly dry up like a spring
But won't be barren like the Gobi
My essence and blood will be suddenly frozen at a critical point
But I won't lose my life as a result
Aah, morning star
Why do you come to light up my dawn

#5

Skyscrapers
Are killers
Repeatedly dismembering life
The solidity of concrete makes me hate
I'm disgusted by the dense forest-like growth of these buildings
The wind was long ago dismembered without a breath or a sound
The western-style suit is thin
No wind to rumple it
Some people die
Some are reborn
The skyscraper's hardheartedness is like durian
You can't describe
The indescribable
Also the heart of impudence
Murder and being murdered
Making a living and being a parasite
Skulking like a net at the lowest level of the city

#6

My wineglass smashes
Whom do my eyes swollen from tears distress
In eternal night on which street corner should I grieve
For whom should my wine be poured
Streetlights repeatedly going on and off
But one after another the streets are still so strange
Aah, lovers
Are you still listening
Does my perpetual drunkenness still move you
Ring roads wreath you
Even drunk you can't fight the tide
The double yellow line is an impassable wall
You cannot change lanes and drive into the distance
Rooftop ads are pompous and elevated
But can be smeared or changed at will anytime
Aah, wine
Please keep knocking me down drunk
Let me be like the repeatedly clipped roadside plants and flowers
Never again able to make out
An original disposition

#7

It ought to return to the nest
That bird of mine that's built an abode on the deck
Tonight's rain
Don't come too early again
Wetting my long-awaited sound of home
The echo of this concrete will make the heart hurt
Will make it hard to forget this life in the city
Gently preserve the tears
Sit long before the window listening
I hear
Distant police sirens tear through the night
I see
Emaciated buildings make the wind blow aslant

#8

Night
Time and again the bar door makes me heavier
The alcoholic scent of the city confuses me
Who wants to wander the streets every day
Gentle music silences me
An indiscernible melody makes me anxious
Faces
Made misty
The wind under the door
Blows cold the soles
Aah, eternal night
Let me lift a glass to you
For me you ward off wind-frost night after night
Aah, eyeglasses
Let me applaud you
Time and again you mistake the direction
Aah, wine
Let me drink freely to you
My roaming is the roaming of wine

#9

It's daybreak
I should check my bags
Can't forget that slender bamboo staff
The wind on the streets will be boiling hot
By bridges rain will fly up
On the roads vehicles will race
And by gates dogs will go wild
People in Starbucks will look askance
Longhaired girls will get flustered
Aah, bamboo staff
Please accompany this sorry wanderer
That alley, a hundred times and I still can't make it out
That lobby, a hundred times and I still dare not enter
That girl, a hundred days and I still dare not look up
Eternal night, a hundred times
and I still don't want a clear head

#10

The city's flowers
Really bloom the same bright red
Who's haggard over you
In your withered early winter
Scraps of paper
Are always drifting down from skyscrapers
Lightly pressing down your stamen
Like a dog
Forever traversing the street
Tramping to bits your dog shit of a life
An autumn chill
Will suddenly descend against the wind
Tearing to pieces the red
Then
Indifferent
I can't judge
In which season to await you
At which dawn to let rain do the watering
Then
Impossible to speak of pain
Impossible to speak of cold

#11

I want to be moved by myself
My journey is packed with hardships
My heart has long been exiled by me
The prosperity of this era can no longer excite me
My heart has long been crying over me
Crying over my lonely struggle with the city
I hate all I want to hate
I detest the life I detest
Like a lone wolf wildly running along a fence
The warm scent of this city no longer calms me

#12

The sky
Finally goes dark
Aah, people
I will play and sing on the square
My guitar is made of poplar from Tianshan Lake
Please listen if it's melodic enough
My low notes sing for the birds of heaven
Aah, people
Please wait for her fragrance
I know the sound of my song will frighten you
Just as your din will fluster me
So celebrate my loss of voice
This roaming in the city has long since led me to despair
Every gaze leads me to resist
Each outline of a back makes me desolate
I simply want to suddenly drop from a high note
I simply want to lie on the street like stakes of leg skin

#13

If
I were a kite flown high by you
Who would look up
Who could build a bow
To shoot that silvery-gray sunlight
I know
Even if I break string and go
I can't fly over this city's high walls
The bridges will shoot me down
Leaving me to rot in a muddy pond
Even if I fly a million miles
There will be skyscrapers to break my wings
You cannot hide from these cities and their murders
You cannot yield to these skyscrapers and their cruelty

#14

Dreams
An iron-hard awakening
The roads outside the window
Have long seemed to wriggle like worms
Open books are strewn about
I can't make sense of words, and am in no position to break lines
No way to speak the long sigh of the heart
I dare not start this day's roaming
This alley
Is bound to have loiterers
Bellow the threshold my grass awaits my watering
This overpass
Is bound to be decked out
My guitar waits in my bosom for my chant
This city
Is bound to have wanderers
Spurning the city and spurned by the city

#15

Smiling falsely
Like a van Gogh painting
Rudely tossed by carnal desire
This city is flawlessly distorted
Similarly I can't truly write my heart
Nor clearly explain my life
My roaming is similarly suspicious
My plaint likewise needs textual criticism
Aah, people
Let me scuttle through the streets like a dog in heat
Let me shock people like a low thief
Like a back-blowing wind I go against the flow in the city
Aah, people
My city is different from yours

#16

I have contemplated death
A hundred times thought of an end to wandering
Days of living for life make me sneer inside
The city I dare not flee confuses people
At its bustling base alone I grieve
Watching the crowd from afar I dare not weep
Aah, hands
Pointing high at red lights, repeatedly give out hatred
I am closely caged by this city
All I acquire makes me repentant
All death moves me
Every leaf makes me utter a million curses
As if tearing at the fractures of my nerves
Aah, city
Whose soul doesn't seem crazed
Whose life doesn't seem vagrant
Whose smiling face doesn't seem a mask
And whose heaven doesn't seem an exile

33

#17

The city is resplendent
Every day surprises me
The buildings walk the streets with me
Concrete and glass together with me are stirred layer upon layer
Together with me the red flowers will be broken
With the city's eternal night creeping in corners
These glorious days make me feel degraded
The mass of this city makes me anxious
Aah, city
This tiny existence ought to distress somebody
This vulnerable life ought to be led by somebody

#18

Spilled like concrete
Streetside I will slowly solidify
People, come clear me away
My obstinacy will vex you
You go high
I want humble
I'd rather crawl on the ground like grass
This scruffy existence makes me free
I won't fight for sunlight in the cracks of buildings
And don't want the moonlight to illuminate my long night
My life
     is
        my life
My roaming
     is
        my roaming
My pride
     is
        my pride
My death
     is
        my death

#19

Trees
Planted in rows
Openly surrounded by skyscrapers
Lamplight
Strikes leaves in innumerable ways
Leaves
Tightly closed eyes unable to cry out
I am arranged by the city
Like a tethered dog, I self harm
Some people watch me
Some are watched
Who wants to interpret the flash of a notion I've just exposed
An array of bridges comes over
An array of confusing curves
Again I'm rearranged by the city
Like a leaf that dies young
Unable to rot on a concrete surface

#20

Time
So accurate it makes one heavy
Do you still remember the day you started to cry
It surely was when you first fell into the city's trap
Instant helplessness like a long street, its end out of sight
Facing the hustle and bustle you make yourself ugly
I stick close to streets like spiderwebs
I am another quarry of this city
Winds will not touch me, but I want to be dazed by blown sand
Rain will not drown me, but I want to be drenched
There are no high walls, but the heart dares not travel far
In the black night I fearfully turn on all lights
Like the city's lamb every day I'm put out to pasture
Repeatedly loitering in bars and vestibules
Aah, city
You hit my heart with alcohol
Who could think of wandering

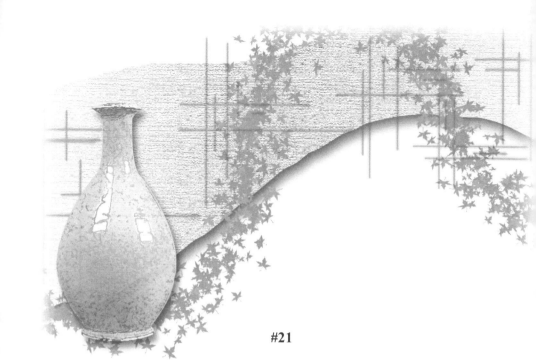

#21

Spinning down
Perfectly received by concrete
No time to wash the whole heart white
Before vanishing underfoot
The snow of the city
Like a strange thought
Utterly endlessly drifting
And absolutely silently perishing
My wine is not yet hot
Outside my window no plum blossoms bloom
Who murdered the snow
Let my streets always be filthy
That sorry tree has just been wet by snow
And in a blink roasted by streetlights
Aah, people
Please look at me standing streetside disconsolate
Tires repeatedly splash muddy water on me

#22

My flute has fractured
A crowd of onlookers finally disperses
This song of roaming is sung time and again
But listeners don't applaud me
Looking askance at their backs, I depart cursing
This solo performance drives people mad
A thousand times wanting to be consoled, to have my face wiped clean
Maybe
A gentle kiss can make me break off roaming
Like the last wanderer of the twenty-first century
My stubbornness confuses me
Like the last wild dog on this city's streets
My life also makes me feel absurd
Aah, flute
Quick with me play the music higher and higher

#23

I'm familiar with *Encountering Sorrow*[1]
I'm familiar with that age-old song of complaint
Yet the days in this city duplicate me
Copying that ancient wandering
Me and myself pity me
Pity this twenty-first century wandering of the heart
These abstruse buildings also infuriate me
And all living beings make me unfamiliar
Aah, *falling blossoms*[2]
In a city without an autumn of gold, how should I fall
When all life is in its pomp you renounce yourself
At a time of gold and green splendor, you're afraid
In carnal desire you have sunk
When low you've felt low
While regretting grudges you've been repentant
Aah, falling blossoms
Who will pity your ache of only wanting to roam

---

[1] A long poem written by Qu Yuan (ca. 339-ca. 278 B.C.E.), China's first named poet.

[2] A play on the poet's penname, Luo Ying, which has the exact sound as the characters translated as "falling blossoms," a phrase frequently found in classical poetry and a conscious echo of its use in "Encountering Sorrow."

24

Sitting in a lobby looking out through glass
My shattered image overlaps cars on the street
My eyes are sliced into five sections
Some are on street corners
Some on chests
Who is me
Who will be simply judged by me
Changing shape innumerable times in a great hall
These changeable days make one uneasy
Facing one's self repeatedly disgusted
Only feeling hypocritical about one's smile
This murky life like the night of the city
Can't say it's bright
Can't say it's dark
The city wanders me
Making me seem like a second wife
loitering in front of the window
The city poisons me
Making me seem a loose woman
intoxicated by opium
The city castrates me
Making me seem gay but constantly sweating
Who is me
My eyes are already sliced into five pieces

#25

Like the sorrowful Qu Yuan,[3] I also lament
Without fragrant thoroughwort how should I dress
The dawn of the city does not reveal a crystalline sparkle
The dusk of the city also has no kitchen smoke
A wandering life on the streets is without flowers to waft fragrance
This steadfast roaming breaks the heart
Is this bustling multitude of life similarly ruthless
Are the gazes of people similarly cold
Who can interpret roaming that is roaming for the sake of roaming
Who can savor distress that is distress for the sake of distress
Who's willing to act as a door
Repeatedly opened and closed
Who's willing to be like a drum
Repeatedly beaten to a pulp and still hoarsely howling
Caught ten thousand times, then quickly fleeing
This pastureland of the soul is bare of grass
Disdained ten thousand times, yet I quickly go roving
This ridge of thought has long been sterile
People who don't love me
Aah, there's no need to be flustered
Your city is not my heaven

---

[3] China's first named poet (C. B.C. 340 - B.C. 278)

#26

I know
Philosophy is already dead
Starbucks is full of low thought
The city precisely defines each person
Defined so that every kind of program can be reset
Wind doesn't speak to wind
Windows watch windows
Shocked in a city without soil
In a flash
The heart is stripped of clothes
And my philosophy
Where should you bury it
Who wants to come weep
Standing streetside barefoot
Crazy in a city without Nietzsche
The wine of this city is like horse piss
Running in a city where thought does not sorrow
This city's roads all seem to lead to a cemetery
Aah, city
You kill my grief

#27

I come to the temple of poetry and look 'round
The laurels are withered beyond recognition
I know
This is another form of the city's murder
The people filling the street guilty of crimes that can't be repaid
I see
They scorch language
Use deformed lines to adorn wedding beds
Repeatedly marry with any groom
Repeatedly accept any trousseau
The poet carnally desires poetry
The city carnally desires the city
The death sentence of the twenty-first century
Who wants to sit on the jury
The degeneration of the twenty-first century
Who wants to take up the banner and resist
Aah, city
I will use poetry to curse your absurdity

#28

The city wall
Tilts into the distance under the evening sun
The road
Has just begun to cool
Sunset clouds slowly approach
Colorful lights abruptly flash on rooftops
Pedestrians are returning home
No more looks into shop windows
A somber flow of traffic moving at snail-pace
Like magma going cold
A tower crane crosses over rooftops
Aiming at my chest with a sheet of steel
The night
Obscures the wall
This wall finally appears rather bleak
Aah, city
Your cold beauty is like alcohol
Impossible to praise
But also impossible to forget

#29

Barefooted walk into the streets
Softly knock on lime-coated walls
My city will exile me
Aah, streets and alleys
Who will now sing and play in your porticos
My wineglass will forsake me
Aah, streets and alleys
Who will now write poetry on your walls
It won't be me now keeping watch for this city at night
Who will inspect the people's doors and windows
It won't be me now wandering for the city
Who will weep over that lost goodness
The person suffering for this city now won't be me
And who will write out those poems on the Milky Way
Naked
As the heart
Staring back lingeringly at you, this city

#30

Finally wanting to sleep
After the beating of a rain shower
Intoxicated by the calm of the whole city
Rain
Makes the streets appear filthy no more
A third-quarter moon
Still rises
A few stars and lights flash together
Late-returnees drunk
Leaning against skyscrapers gruffly sing
A breeze
Blows back and forth
Setting saplings to swaying
I don't see leaves drop
But see raindrops go yellow as they fall
Dodging the rain a feral cat shivers
Shaking the yellow rain onto tree roots
Aah, city
I enter paradise together with you

Impressions
(A Sequence of Fourteen Poems)

Walls

Folded
Up
See me
Unable to break through
From day to night
In a corner
Cowering
My back
Tightly propped
Moonlight
Finally shoots over
Illuminating
Me
And
Walls

Bridges

Burn me
Like
The resistance of donkeys
Feet painfully
Tramp
As if
Walked on by dogs
An arbitrary gaze into the distance
Vehicles
Approach
Wheeling up
Later
I
Spiral down
Like days
Repeatedly burnt
This
Fucking dog of a bridge
Burns me again

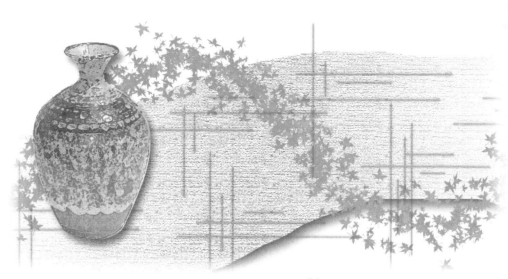

Noon

The trees
Sway no more
The heart
Dare not rely on
Fear
To know
Then
Piss together
Beer
Drunk
Carefully
Then
Drunk again
See ants
Rush up
Then
Trampled
Noon
A murder plot underway
Avoid being murdered
Then carry out murder
Noon
Wind
Suddenly burning hot

Dawn

A fishy-smelling night
Recedes
Sunlight
Dyes red
The peaks of roofs
The streets
Will noisily surge
Man
And
Dog
Will cascade into early morning
Dawn
Will be like a horse's buttocks
And be whipped
The streets
Formerly dirtied
Again dirtied
Dawn
Stands up
Waited for and watched
Then
Stripped clean again

Streetlights

Chilled
By the night wind
Like eyes
Coldly scanning
Not at all anxious
A thick night
Repeatedly
Pushed back
By the streets
The heart
Chillily passes by
And doesn't intend
To peek at anybody
Slowly button up
Clothes
Like a girl tightly shielding
Her breasts
Savagely stared at
By streetlights
Just like a dog
Having its back broken

Bus Stop

Separated
By streetlights
Looking into the distance
Is effortless
Lazily
Carrying on
People
Seemingly coming and going
Making
The bus stop
Dither
Eyes
Gazed at
Surreptitiously
The hundredth woman
Can't be clearly seen
But the bus stop
Can't
Pass by again
Like a dung bucket
It's hammered to bits
By me

Bars

Limping at an angle
A drunk
Dims
Me
With a lamp
Makes a bench
From my hands
A dogskin drum
Worn and loose
Is excreted
Duplicated
Heart-movingly
A cigarette
Approaches
Easily
Burning
Violets
To hell with his
Ball game
Change stations
And a woman
Is pointing
At a man's
Part

Statues

Like
Urban
Feral dogs
Indifferent to gender
Living together
On a square
Not daring to draw near
The sunlight
Angling and long
Passersby
Are admired
Into anxiety
Fleeing
The return looks
Of mongrels
The air
Is sourly
Sent back
Like
A gold-plated
Length
Offending the eye
Pigeons
Fly in again
And are again
Glued
To the ground

Rainy Days

Lightly
As
Weeping willow branches
Are slender
The water
Pierced
Dark red
The broken
Sigh
The streets
Humbly
Silent
Scatter
People
Like
Dog shit
Under trees
Grass
Suspiciously
Quivers
Like
A shared plot
With rainy days
Making
The ground
Desolate
Directly
Striking
My heart

Pets

Like me
By
The city
Reared in a pen
A metallic
Hatred
Fantasies
Like horse piss
Every day
Wanting
To shatter
Sunlight
Behind
The back
Of the curses
Of time pieces
Naked
Casting off
Candlelight
Like lead wire
Like
Seamless lightning
Rolling past
Then
Melting into
A soup of mud

Web Addresses

Like
Iron
Fused
Randomly
Stacked
Beside the street
Trichromatic
Scintillations
Will sound
Like
Sawn-off
Looks
Approaching
Shallow
Responses
Stopped
Above a sewer drain

Morning Crows

Lowly
Thieves
Dart by
The pond
And
Fly across it
The girls
Of willow wood
Caw
Like
Sludge
Stuck tight
To your back
Coarse
Mouths
Black and long
Like
All
Dastardly lives
Stealing
Through
A mucky thicket
Making
A screen
Of
Filth
So
Low
It's like
Dewdrops
Noiselessly
Wetting
Clothes

Doorbells

Just like my
Helplessness
Inadvertently
Rung
Like
My weariness
Oozing everywhere
In
The city
Then
Doing it
Again
Silently
Facing up
To
Doors
Refusing
Sunlight
Refusing
To be
Repeatedly
Rung
Like
A sheet-iron flower
Broken off
Then
Soldered back on

An Orchestra

Like feral cats
In the city
Cheaply sold
At night
In heat
Against the lights
A drum set
Thumped
Lasciviously
Like
An evil-minded
Prostitute
As if
Caterwauling
Rationally
In the city
Like
A century
Selling sex
In the city

Impressions of Me on Myself
(A Sequence of Sixteen Poems)

Introduction

I'm me
And I am not me

#1

Dreaming
And also
Rotting
Hidden
Like an angle iron
And I do not go
To be
Screwed on
To a scaffold
After being cut off
Like
A pig
Being
Frozen in
An icebox

#2

A long-range
Greed
After
A
Rust-colored
Image
A road
For cockroach
Feet
Polluted
By
Purple
A likeness
Of
Underwear
Getting colors mixed up
In the laundry room

#3

The likeness
Of
A curtain
At midnight
Suddenly
Torn
Cowering
Not knowing
What to do
Leaping into
The flower
Garden
Deer
Are
Mating
Tree trunks
Fishy smelling
Like
Saliva
Drowning
All
Paths

4

Stacked
Doors
Exit
Enter
Barring
Bats
Thieving love
Lewd
Hearts
Open
Nets
Twisted to tatters
The remnants of walls
Hands
Coiling
Bridges
Throwing into disorder
Grassy banks
At midnight
Like wolves
Steel hard
Cutting across
The square

5

Looking
With hatred
At coffee
An obstinate
Aroma
Wanting
To howl wildly
Like a dog
A tightly held
Table leg
Like fish
Easily
Burning
The hand
Language
Baked hot
Like
Wine
Splattering
Line by line
Then
Ice
Cold

 # 6

Evaded
Days
Come
Back
Again
Like cymbals
Struck
At similar
Lengths
Cast off
Eyes
Don't go
Under
The table
Wandering
Nobody
Hates me
And pierces
My throat
With
A golden hairpin
Far-off
Iron
Cooling
Down
Like
A trap
Laid out
By a woman
At dawn

7

Living
Like
Double-layer tissue paper
Also
Despised
By
Philosophy
Shelled
Like a bean
Pod
A
Dried-out
Helplessness
Chopped off
Legs
Still
Don't hurt
Anaesthetized
Beyond any meaning
Like
A light
Finally switched off
The night is black
Everything
Is
Quiet

8

Too lazy
To again
Want to
Resist
The door
Of the years
Will not
Be knocked on
Down
At
The bottom
Of a trap
Shout
You cannot
Be forgotten
By
The hunter
Like
A thumbtack
Pressed into
A wooden wall
Silently
Rusting
Also possibly
Burning
The
Raised
Iron
Still
Smashes in
Inaccurate
Directions

9

Leapt over
Again
And
Again
By
Bridges
Water
Like
A cinnabar stove
Refines me
Just so
Dull
An agitated
Face
Very long
Stained
By
Fish
Feces
Gazing up
From
Water's bottom
Like
Sunken wood
Half dim
Half heavy
In an instant
Struck
By
A falling stone
Me
And
Me
Just like
Lines on the water
Circle on circle
Changing shape

10

Quiet
Enough
To frighten
Oneself
Under
The brightest
Lamp
Distracted
Like
Light
Arriving
Over eight million years
So tired
Not wanting
To penetrate
The vestibule
Waiting
To be murdered
Like a hedgehog
Playing dead
Like
Long hair
Inch by inch
Wrung
Off
Then
Inch by inch
Swept away

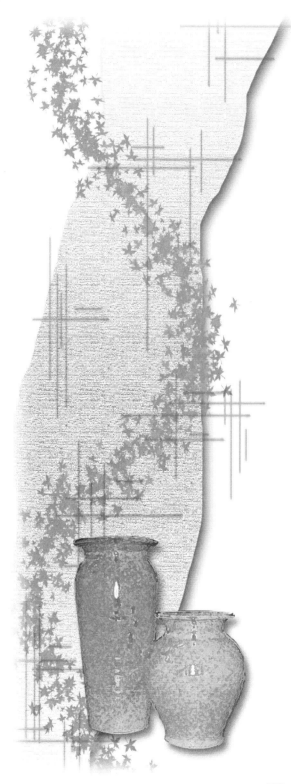

11

Like
A
Faded
Painting
Fixed
On
A wall
The manner in which
The wind blows
Odd
And
Hard to dodge
Bare-bottomed
Nails
Pester me
Beams of light
Like
Airborne blades
Fly in
Upside down
A one-eyed
Person
Enters
And is then
Easily
Imprisoned
My faded color
Revolts against
My
Motley shade
The rain
Comes down so
It makes
The heart race

12

Merge
On
The tracks
Then
Wait for the terminus
To stretch out
Designed
To submit
Like
Rotten bamboo in tight rolls
Weak
Yet
Solid
Back to
The city
Like
A stinking
Calabash
Mutually exclusive
Light
From other than the sun
Namelessly
Shines
Yet
Leaves me
Utterly
Unmoved

13

A heart
Washed clean
Deep red
Distracting thoughts
And
Relaxed
Eyes
Used
To see people
Then
Disdainfully look
Like
A boomerang
Sent
Out
With deadly accuracy
The bastards
Will
Approach
And
Deeply regret it
The wind shear
Shattered
Doors
Raped
By
A bed-wetting

14

Let
A river
Flow
Out of
A deep
Fog
Contra rotating
Hands
Leap
Boundless
Like
A shameless
Leech
City lights
Also
Flash sporadically
Like
Ringing
In the ears
Like
Raised
Eyebrows
Struck
By
A tile
Willow catkins
Fly up
Like
An inescapable
Pain
An easily accomplished
Occupation

 # 15

Rain
On the left side
Like
Titanium alloy
Cold and hard
Well-defined edges
A nude form
Wrapped
In clothes
And
In pain
The remnant
Of a yell
Like
A worm
Being
Crushed
Out of
Hatred
And
Resolve
The anus
Inflexibly
Resists

16

It's impossible
To wipe
Yourself
From
Your
Memory
Singing
With
A thousand tons
Of gold
Cannot
Grow the value
Of
The heart
A city's
Rainbow
Certainly doesn't count
As pure and fresh
Flowers fall
To
Earth
The dying die
The living live
From
Rooftop corners
Shooting
The city's
Light
Into
The streets
Like
Meat
Stripped of bones
Striated
Melting
A lit
Flame

11

Going over a wall
Traversing
The alleys
Of half the city
Half dark
Half bright
Gates
Half shut
By wind
Tears
Half running
From people

Drawers

It's as if my distress
Was being casually pulled open
Then carelessly closed
It was born on my back from my distant homeland
Like grains of wheat in the seams of a bag
Unexpectedly scattered on a table
Abruptly I want to lean in close against your chest
Like a child dreaming of a mother's breasts
Standing at the summit, I daren't look back
The splendor of this city fills my eyes with tears
Far off
A bright mountain is going wild
In front of a lamp
My girl is dressing and making up
Aah, wind
Why have you mistakenly knocked at my window again

On the Road

I admit
I cannot resist the pleasure of carnal desire
And the shame of poverty has left me speechless
The innocence of this wandering wearied me long ago
The Milky Way of this city long ago left me alone
My heart is sometimes hurt, sometimes dull
Lost in the streets it feels safe
The streetlights passed are forgotten, and then I walk again
The people sworn at are forgotten then cursed again
The doors knocked at are forgotten then knocked at again
And roads fled down are forgotten then fled down again
Without a companion I must still wander
From where will a city not wandered gain glory
How are the skyscrapers of a city frozen solid
How are the streets of a city endless
Forget it
Anyway, I have only the road

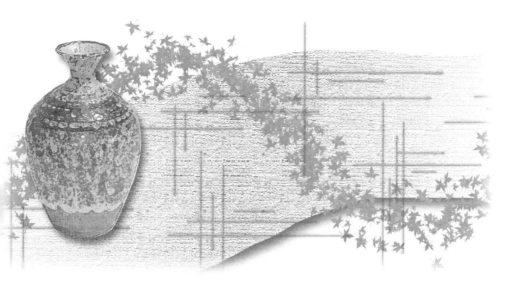

Shorthaired Girl

Show windows under streetlights like water
Reflect me ruthlessly
A short, shallow affection suddenly appears
The short is black hair like tenderness at the bottom of the heart
Moved by a show window
A face-off where eyes need not meet
Cheering for the indifference of beauty
A love that need not be spied on
Like tenderness refracted by a show window
The heart trembles then walks away

The Windows of a Skyscraper

It seems every window of the skyscraper is flashing
Looking up expecting to see somebody's smiling face appear
I'm too lonely, like the city's buildings looking coldly upon each other
Too helpless, like city love easily negated
Leaning back against a streetlight, I repeatedly imagine the gentle fra-
grance
The illusory lover makes my mood flicker
Footsteps will come and go, dense and heavy
The gaze up will be long, even to infinity
Like windows, a few open, a few closed
Like people, some tender, some strange
Like loves, some doubtful, some dependable
Like kisses, some heavy, some icy
Among skyscrapers
Who will wet their eyes for me

82

Gray Windows

The wooden window trembles
Half open and gray
The heart is heavy
Nocturnal thoughts while half awake
In front of a lamp reading poetry
Half obscure, half bitter
Shadows of trees shake
Half showing, half hidden, very dramatic
The sound of a bell half distant
Low and rising, like murder with a concealed weapon
Both eyes half wet
No need to look 'round, all is deeply seen

Living

Living
Is like a streetside tree, withered yet green
Leaned on repeatedly
Then adrift season after season
A sentimental dog comes again and again
On unchosen days
I'm fixed in place by its yellowy-brown piss
Dry and hard like a repeatedly used passion
Even the dog finds it hard to endure an inescapable caress
The heart's bitterness is peeled off layer by layer like bark
Living
Is to clench teeth and swear not to speak of pain

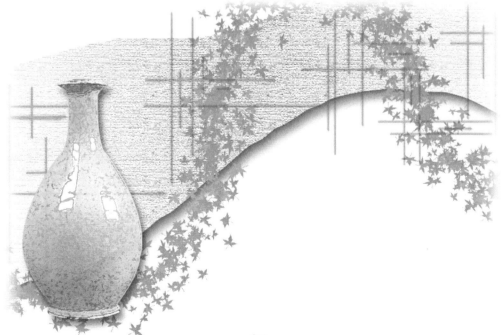

A Fine Moonlit Night

I will think of you, fine moonlit night
And be your seventeenth lover
I will
Paint eyebrows under a tilting lamp
Make my face for the seventeenth type of kiss
The wall I'm leaning on will remain firm
The seventeenth sort of waiting is not at all out of shape
Like the seventeenth good moon lights things up
Like the city's seventeenth type of bastard
Fine moonlit night, I'll wait for you
For your seventeenth sort of approach

85

A Railing Leaned Upon

Who has leaned on my railing
Waiting for an evening breeze to lazily swirl in
Coldly gazing at the splendor of the city's lights
Indifferently preparing for another spell of solitude
Wind in the city pledges no love to mountains or the sea
The railing leaned upon will repeatedly be leaned on
Lazily swirling breezes will repeatedly swirl
A cooled heart will repeatedly cool
And this city's people will be repeatedly strange
Who has leaned on my railing
Whose warmth lingers

The Distances
of the City

The distances of the city
Make me appear and disappear
A deep-set autumn goes faintly purple
Intricate colors are gorgeous
Butterflies and orchids are gently amorous
And the bird of paradise is contented
Hard to voice affection is like a sere chrysanthemum
So pure and yellow, it can't shake a sheet of rain
A helpless waiting like a damaged lotus
So dried out, it can't bear to shiver from cold
The distances of a city
Like frost
Repeatedly wither you

Existence

I've considered my life
I know this city has me hemmed in
Roaming is merely a form of pointless resistance
Thought has long been impoverished to the maddening point
Extravagant and shameless
Injurious and heartless
On chance meeting there are no more tears
On parting there is no more heartbreak
Like the cold glass snuggled up to last night
Abandonment in this city often makes one relax
Like new eyebrows drawn this morning
And life in this city actually makes one calm
Existing
Like an ape reared in captivity by the city

A Foggy Morning

A foggy morning
The streets misty like mountain forests
Walking on tiptoe
Like the hidden shadows in reminiscence
Murky lights flash
Like the heavy departure of an old friend
The wind doesn't come
The haziness of the city comes and goes
People do not return home
This heart's misery is sometimes heavy, sometimes light
Foggy mornings
You make me want to cry and groan

I'm a Returning Insect

I'm a returning insect
Crawling in the dusk of the city
The city raised me
I die when it's time to die
Live when it's time to live
On love
Confused and interchangeable

I softly sing like a cricket in a jar
The process of mating is simple and transparent
I will be soundless like a cockroach behind the door
The trail of the love hunt is both tense and calm
The return to the city has nothing to do with the season
Passing in variety
Existing in odd shapes
As degenerate as this city
As fatuous as these days
Winter insects are like summer grass, neither fish nor fowl
Crossbreeding in the city's concrete jungle
As it's impossible to be accepted by this city
My nastiness will revolt people

No Choice But

There's no choice but to live in the city
No choice but to think of people no longer loved
Moved by the drop of a leaf
Worried about the city's disorder
There's no choice but to be rich and speak fellow-feeling
No choice but to be cultured and speak of status
Feeling bad about interminable rain
Regretting a hypocritical heart
There's no choice but to hurt people already hurt
No choice but to curse people already cursed
Solemn for the autumn fall of chrysanthemums
Deeply hurt by the indifference of emotions

Like a casually sent rubbish SMS
I've no choice but to scurry about the city's net

No Rain This Morning

No rain this morning
Alleys without umbrellas are desolate
Angling, extending roads are without dust
People opposite are crossing speechless
I see a ray of sun shoot in
Which family's girl has her coat blown open
A navel ornament flashing silver
Wandering I pass through a stretch of pure fragrance
Lazily walking past compound walls
I see pigeons squatting on tiles

No rain this morning
In front of a gate a kitten basks in the sun

I Must Know

I must know
Do I still have to calmly copulate
I must know
Have I really not been cloned
Has my name truly been called
Has my wife really not changed sex
Are the people under the lights truly not going to bite me
Has my dog really not sneeringly said
Bastard
You're merely one deadbeat in this city

Life Like an SMS

Life is like an SMS
Delivered without a known name
It's neither particularly long
Nor particularly short
Also, neither distant nor close
Repeatedly sent in batches but not knowing why
And read with insufficient emphasis
Who will believe the pain that's related
Left out like trash, interesting nobody

Life like an SMS
Cheap without any real cost

Midnight Streets

At midnight, the heart can finally start to go wild
Arbitrarily penetrating alleys and randomly getting lost
Tightly closed doors and windows no longer a worry, will suddenly
open
Playfully flashed warmth will leave you unable to bear the sorrow
The night breeze is so still, you are forced to reminisce
At midnight, I freely allow my heart to be desolate
And finally start to seriously consider this city
Under the lights' shadows, eventually seeing an appearance of beauty

There's the flash of a white cat on the lawn
Like a blade ruthlessly slicing my eyelids to shreds

The Love of Alcohol

It's me punishing the night once more
The pain of a hangover lets me enjoy a different kind of happiness
I don't know if I've again said something dirty
In wild dreams alcohol is my sole companion
The thought of sorghum spirits and I can't resist getting drunk nightly
The thought of an oil lamp and the wine in my glass already piping hot
When you can't think of anything, you're lying in the wine
And an evil wind will cool your spine

Aah, interminable night
For you I pour glass after glass

A Street Corner

The streets roll under the sunlight of the city
Once more the horizon is halted by a traffic light
Looking back and up through concrete skyscrapers
I can't see who's been forgotten in the starry sky
Inventorying my helplessness is both crooked and long
I can't enter the building
Can't exit a show window
I give my regards to myself in the shadows of lights
And the wind sweeps off my clothes
Standing on a brick street corner, I dare not turn

To a Stranger

A chance meeting on a little bridge
Narrow like a channel of emotion impossible to get 'round
The smile before the retreat like the sound of a flute
Its remote air beautiful and tender
This sudden impulse is like the plucking of a string
Soft, tearless sobs follow the trills of an overture
The distance of strangeness is like heart's desolate calm
A desiccated delusion is fragrant in the most distant places

Not Allowed

You're not allowed to love me
My heart is only left disconsolate
Your black hair is not allowed to flutter
You're not allowed to caress my sight
My cricket sings out of loneliness
Please don't let the wind knock down its sound
Please don't ask about the dewy grass
Only it knows the whereabouts of fallen leaves
You're not allowed to love me
My heart is as calm as lake water
When spring returns, I'm enchanting
When snow drifts, I'm sealed up by the cold
Allowing you come and go in a rush
At autumn harvest, you have fruit
In early summer, you're fragrant
What can be had, I let you have
What can be lost, I'll not retain
Let me censor all dreams
Let the world flourish with weeds like a wasteland
Let misery breed misery
As soon as you've had it, innocence is unnecessary
Let me gently forget you
You're not allowed to love me
Your tears are not allowed to dampen my mind
You're not allowed to touch my loneliness
You're not allowed to stand in my dreams
Like a police box in an intersection
Frozen yet impossible to move

A Cold Current

The cold current is back again
Standing in the cold gloom of the courtyard
Like a visitor who's knocked at the wrong door
In a blink life goes in a wrong direction
The heart cools, rapidly reducing its temperature at mid-
night
In days at the beginning who can say
When hearts built defensive lines
The composition of tales from the past warp
When people stand silently, confronting each other
Who can distinguish gain and loss
The cold current is back
Wearing an icy cotton gown
Like a girl startled awake while sleepwalking
But the terror wears a smile

Did You Once Have a Dream

When you opt for your tender feelings
Your beautiful hair isn't allowed to quiver
O, I ask you
Did you once have a dream
A cloud, never able to drift
When you garner your grief
Your teardrops aren't to glisten
O, I ask you
Did you once have a dream
A breeze, never to be gathered in
When I leaf through your lethargy
Your smiling face isn't to lose heart
O, I ask you
Did you once have a dream
A song, never to be finished being sung
When I walk out of your memory
Your name isn't to be reprinted
O, I ask you
Did you once have a dream
One sentence, it can never be clearly heard

Girl

Let me drop down beside you
A quiet laugh because of your get-up
Causes you to lift up longings
humped back over a long distance
Page after page bound in your study
The yearning mind brilliant as a rainbow
Passes through eternal night,
is put up high in your sky
Day by day I will stride over toward you
And stand watch
before your windownsoftly singing
Girl
Please be pretty, please be fragrant

Outside the Window

A clear dawn and distant mountains
Flat as in a dream
Lamplight
A final peace
Early-rising morning mist spreads
A lover's soft whispered words
Make an inventory of the long night
The unloaded memory is a pale red

Postscript

As a poet who lives in present-day China, I couldn't help but have all sorts of feelings in my mind.

The urbanization process in the West has been steady, while the criticisms and introspections toward the common customs of mankind and the pursuit for material goods in the cities appear to be in conventional pattern or impassive. In present-day China, however, no one will fail to feel dazzled and stunned at the economic development in such a high speed. Accompanying the economic development are the fierce conflicts between the traditional value and modern value, and as a poet, I can feel the pains of inner division of life and the necessity of thinking. It is impossible to feel the artistic conception as described by traditional poems. Urbanization has brought about wealth and impulsiveness, the covered poverty and distortion, which has propelled the society to change in redoubled speed.

I am a beneficiary of urbanization, a beneficiary of China's social and economic development. But as a poet, I have never got rid of the puzzlement in the failure to control my own soul and any other things. All this makes people in high spirits and excitement. My poetry collection is a reflection of my soul in the process. I hope it will be in harmony with the swiftly changing society in China, its culture and value, and the possible vitality of present-day poems in China.

To speak frankly, in my view, the present-day poems in the world are generally in the tendency of inwardly, self-entertaining, and self-love style writing by petty writers—petty men and petty women. Such writings are actually a kind of way to act as a spoiled child by unbosoming oneself, a kind of way to act as a spoiled child in public and facing the readers. It is hard for me to tell where the factors are brewing that will make the present-day poems with shocking, pounding, and communicating strength. But it is my opinion that all poets have the responsibility to jointly seek it so the present-day poems will provide a possible spiritual height in a society, which is becoming more and more materialized and for the mankind, who is more self-oriented, and that will make the complicated world appear not too ugly.

As to the translation and publication of the collection, I should thank Dorrance Publishing Company, who was able to pick up the poems from the present-day Chinese poems twinkling in the mist and has paid great efforts to edit and publish them. I hope this collection of poems will provide an opportunity to promote the communication and exchange of modern poems between the United States and China in a deep way. I also want to thank Mr. Michael Day for his meticulous translation of the poems. As far as I know, he has translated many poems into English from poets who represent the modern Chinese poems. Therefore, my appreciation is not only for his help to me, but also for his remarkable contribution to modern Chinese poems.

I am also grateful for my friends Mr. Tang Xiaodu and Xi Chuan. Both of them are tireless explorers, observers, critics of modern Chinese poems, and promoters for the exchange of modern poems between China and other countries. The Zhongkun Pamirs Literature Workshop led by them is playing an ever important role in this field, and both of them have paid great attention to the collection's translation and publication.

Finally, I wish to express my special thanks to my friend Mr. Gao Ping, his partner, Ms. He Jingxiu, and my assistant, Xu Hong. Their efforts to get this collection published in the U.S. have made me feel deep in my heart the importance of friendship.

I will watch with a kind of uneasiness how my readers respond to my collection. In any case, I should thank all who had the patience to read this page.

Luo Ying
November 3, 2006